SUMMARY:

The Operator

Firing the Shots that Killed Osama bin Laden

and My Years as a SEAL Team Warrior

ABBEY BEATHAN

Legal & Disclaimer

Table of Contents

The Book at a Glance

Concluding a total of four hundred combat missions including the daring rescue for the "Lone Survivor" Marcus Luttrell in the Taliban-controlled Korengal "Death Valley"; saving Captain Richard Phillips during the *Maersk Alabama* hijacking; and the shots that killed the world's most wanted terrorist Osama bin Laden, Robert "Rob" O'Neill recounts his thrilling, action-packed, and humor-filled experiences as a Navy SEAL operator.

This book, aptly named *The Operator*, will open the eyes of its readers about the bravery and selflessness of soldiers who sacrifice their lives to pave the way for peace and to show us the meaning and consequence of heroism.

As a young boy from Butte, Montana, it never crossed Rob's mind to join the military, much less the elite Special Forces: the Navy SEALs. Still, the sense of perseverance was ingrained in Rob by his father and when it was time to choose and tread his own path, determination led him. Rob enlisted for the Navy and rigorously trained himself with discipline.

He found himself passing the arduous Navy SEALs screening test as one of four from the five hundred examinees. He enlisted in the BUD/S Class 208 which made the screening test seem like a vacation. Known for its infamous obstacles and tests, termed "evolutions", the BUD/S did not only require a strong physique but a strong mind and will which will not bend to any pressure.

BUD/S Hell Week was designed to make trainees suffer and resign to failure, hence its name. Even as men around him continued to break and give up, Rob refused to crack under the stress of training against the huge forceful ocean waves, daunting obstacle courses, the frigid cold, strenuous physical tests, the weight of rubber rafts, lack of sleep, body pain, and screaming instructors. He graduated with the best from the best as an official Navy SEAL.

In his days as a SEAL amidst the al-Qaeda and Taliban terrorism threat, Rob would learn many things as a soldier and as a man. He formed bonds and great friendships with his crewmates as they stared death in the face in every mission. Rob also joined the historic squadron Team X (blacked out for confidentiality) whose men would inspire him to become a great leader and a hero. Rob survived many life-threatening situations during his several deployment missions in Iraq and Afghanistan: facing suicide bombers and IED threats, walking through minefields, fighting hordes of Taliban, jumping in high altitudes, assassinating high-valued terrorists, and blowing up enemy bases. Along the way, Rob would learn to make sacrifices, especially to his beloved family, and see his own brave teammates make their own sacrifices.

Although he deeply mourned the loss of his brothers he treated as family, this would only strengthen his resolve to keep fighting and bring justice to the people who orchestrated the deaths of thousands of innocents. Rob would earn several awards, including a Silver Star for his valor in the battlefield. But, it would almost be ten years before Rob would face the world's most wanted man and the perpetrator of the infamous 9/11 disaster: Osama bin Laden, and would fire the shots that changed the world and made millions of people rejoice.

Chapter One

As a kid, Robert "Rob" O'Neill never really thought about joining the military except during toy gun wars and playing shooter video games in Butte, Montana. He spent his childhood days playing ninja and roof jumping with his friends and his athletic younger sister Kelley. When they moved downtown with his mom, who was divorced with his dad, he was inspired by a Michael Jordan ad which connected to his obsessive drive to keep striving. His father took him to play basketball in nearby courts to push their limits and skills in shooting.

At age twelve, Rob killed his first deer with the same kind of rifle he would eventually use as a SEAL sniper. Any hint of remorse during his first hunts eventually fell away as more hunting seasons followed. By the time Rob shot the prized "six point" bull elk before he turned eighteen, he felt only pride.

It was in the fall of 1994 when he met his first Navy SEAL, Jim. Rob managed to impress him after they climbed straight uphill in the dark with no breaks. Jim told him that he ought to consider becoming a SEAL but Rob, although flattered, never took it seriously.

Hilariously, it was his girlfriend's father who managed to

indirectly convince him to join the military. Drunk and miserable after he discovered that his girlfriend hung out with another boy, Rob barged into his girlfriend's house without fully grasping the consequences. Her Italian father, infamous for his toughness, took pity and merely escorted him out the house. Rob had a realization after that. He didn't want to spend his eternity in the Butte whining and acting like a fool.

Rob was excited by the idea of wearing a cool uniform and impressing the town with some war stories. The possibility of death and combat never came into his mind. On April 1995, Rob went to the Marine recruitment office only to discover that the recruiter wasn't present. The Navy Chief, a bit desperate to fill his quotas, managed to trick the naïve Rob into joining the Navy instead. He immediately enrolled even though Rob did not even knew how to swim.

After quitting his job shoveling rocks in a copper mine facility, Rob went ahead to train himself for the SEAL screening test. Rob was pathetic: he could only manage one pull up and swim a second length before his biceps gave up. Luckily, a high school friend taught him basic swimming techniques. Every day, he swam on the school pool for a few hours, practice his pull-ups, and run. With determination and hard work, Rob got a lot stronger.

On January 28, 1996, Rob officially joined the Navy at the Butte military enlistment processing after a tedious conversation with "The Commander" about quitting marijuana even though he only tried it a year before. His friends and family waved him off the next day in the Bert Mooney Airport with another recruit from his college, Tracy Longmire.

Never did they knew that fifteen years later, that naïve young man would confront the world's most wanted terrorist and fill the D.C. and New York City with cheer.

Chapter Two

Tracy and Rob found themselves boarding a bus filled with "all-knowing" city guys who were confident, if not a bit boastful, about passing the grueling SEAL selection process. Their bravado scared Rob as he eventually started to regret his decision while he watched his fellow recruits getting yelled at by drill instructors.

Boot camp wasn't like the movies. Everybody talked funny because of their different accents and even one recruit from the Philippines couldn't speak English. Instead of crawling under barbed wires and mud, they learned Navy customs, courtesies, cleaning, and lots and lots of folding. If it wasn't folding, the recruits practiced walking and marching which were the only exercise they got. Plus, all their food were covered in gravy.

Scared that he would get fat, Rob immediately signed up for the first SEAL screening test, also called "evolutions." It was a huge mistake since he just got the Navy immunization shots and woke up sick and weak. Rob could barely brush his teeth. He went as far as passing the swimming test but finally gave out with the push-ups. Thankfully, he had two more attempts.

By Thursday, Rob was free from the rest of the vaccination effects. All the hard work from his preparations paid off as he was one of the four recruits who passed the screening test out of five hundred. But that exhausting test was nothing compared to what they're going to face next: the twenty-eight-week Basic Underwater Demolition/SEAL (BUD/S). Still, Rob was happy and excited to go to the Coronado naval base near the famous San Diego beaches to impress the ladies with his SEAL trainee uniform.

After he enlisted, Rob studied the history of SEAL, its origins dating back from the Navy frogmen of World War II. These Underwater Demolition Teams were so effective that the Navy evolved it into guerilla and counter-guerilla units as the first of the Sea, Air, and Land teams. Now, Rob was going to be a part of it.

At least, he would have been. In order to prepare his body for Coronado and stealthily borrow the phones in the pool area, Rob retook the BUD/S screening tests again and again. It was a huge risk: to fail once, even after passing, would cancel his trip. Fortunately, after taking the test ten times, he steadily improved his scores.

Rob chose the Aircrew Survival Equipmentman School in Millington, Tennessee for their post-boot camp training with his close friend, Matthew Parris since it would get them to Coronado the quickest. He never expected that he would enjoy learning to sew parachutes from a massive, muscular Marine. Rob and Matthew trained together, got drunk together, and went back to Butte, Montana together.

On their way to Coronado, Rob read about Richard Marcinko, a SEAL who formed a secret elite strike force specifically designed for terrorists hidden in civilian populations. His brotherhood, called "operators", would ignore the Navy customs and courtesies to achieve maximum effectiveness. Although Marcinko was sent to prison after being charged with government contract fraud, Rob believed that he couldn't judge the man because at the end of the day, his primary focus was his mission and his men.

The pair would finally arrive at Coronado at Thursday dusk. During their first swim in the Pacific Ocean, they watched in awe as seven inflatable rowboats full of BUD/S Class 207 men finished "Around the World", a complete circumnavigation of Coronado Island which they had started since Sunday.

The next day, they checked in as BUD/S Class 208.

Chapter Three

With the barracks still full of Class 205 who were waiting for their graduation, Matthew and Rob were housed in the "X Division" with the men who quit or failed the SEAL training. X Division was full of negativity and know-it-alls who blamed the training and instructors for their failures.

Fortunately for them, the pair was reassigned after a few days to building 602 in the heart of the BUD/S compound. Still, both were unsure of what would happen during the three phases of SEAL training: physical training, diving, and land warfare and demolition. Before they could be assigned to a class, the newcomers had to undergo a few weeks of Physical Training Rehabilitation and Remediation (PTRR), a preliminary training to prepare them for Phase One and give the instructors an opportunity to catch men who were undeserving and ensure that they would never make it further.

Unfortunately, Matthew was one of the men who caught the instructor's attention after he boasted about his experience in the Army boot camp, stating that he was unafraid because he already knew what to expect. The instructor's reaction scared the whole class to the point that Rob peed his pants.

Rob learned quickly though. He realized that making excuses during the exhausting training would only make the mean instructors angrier. Eventually, the PTRR concluded with the same test they had to pass in boot camp. However, some men still failed, including Matthew. After the intense training, he had started to become discouraged and the instructors' targeting just added to the pressure. He was sent to a "review board" who could sentence him to the X Division and a life of mopping. Much to their delight, the hearing officer made Matthew return to class.

They had a ceremony on Friday where they exchanged their five-point navy caps for the BUD/S helmets. Filled with pride, Rob stenciled his name and painted the helmet green, a milestone achieved. He never knew how hard Phase One would be compared to the PTRR.

Before dawn on Monday morning, the trainees were led by their frustrated Officer in Charge, Lt. Mike to the grinder. Rob couldn't blame him for the stress since Mike would receive punishment if the rest of his crew messed up. After finally getting their roll calls correctly, they split into seven-man boat crews to start Phase One. Before they could get to their fins however, the instructors hit them with freezing water from the hoses, sabotaged their head counts, made them sprint a quarter mile to the Pacific Ocean, and ordered them to plunge in the cold waves. They had a special punishment prepared for those who cheated as well. Those who played fair still faced hundreds of various push-ups and ab exercises while getting yelled at by instructors for an hour. Failures would be plunged in ice water.

For breakfast, the trainees had to plunge in the frigid waters, run a mile, fight two hundred others for food, and run back with still enough energy and spirit for a six-mile conditioning run in less than an hour. They were doomed. Yet, Rob refused to give up and let his father, the only one who believed in him, down. He was never going to let his helmet, stenciled with their last name, his father's name, placed in "the quitter line".

Even though the first week was designed to scare and exhaust the recruits, Rob still found good things left in the BUD/S, like the eat-all-you-can food and Instructor A. Instructor A was the complete opposite of the other vile instructors. He motivated people to not quit and became the reason why Rob and so many others made it through. Especially during the obstacle course.

It was the highest and most daunting course for Rob with its fifty-foot-high cargo nets, log-jumping, slide for life, and reverse somersaults. By a few weeks, the trainees started to learn and develop techniques that made the nerve-racking obstacles easier. Unfortunately for Matthew, he learned the technique late as a gust of wind blew at exactly the wrong time. He fell and broke his shoulder. Although he lost his chance in becoming a SEAL, he later became the first rigger on the Navy Parachute Team "Leap Frogs" and an excellent skydiver.

Eventually, Rob started to enjoy the obstacles as he tried to beat the record held by a SEAL named Neil Roberts. Little did Rob knew that Roberts would have an important role in his future.

The remaining trainees faced other tests such as "drown-proofing" where instructors tie their hands and feet together, then toss them to a pool so they could practice bobbing, wriggle-swimming, and retrieving masks at the bottom using only their teeth. Rob personally enjoyed the four-mile timed runs in the sand under twenty-eight minutes. He even won a bet by placing first in one of the runs. But before that, he had to relieve his stress by smoking with Singaporean exchange students. By the end of the BUD/S though, they were running five miles with Rob completing it under fifteen minutes and fifteen seconds.

No one really passes the room inspections at BUD/S. The instructors would always find something dirty in a perfectly clean, immaculate, and organized room, or at least make something dirty. Rob and his roommates had their ceilings sprayed with sand, lockers sprayed with salt water, and boots stepped on. The instructors thought it was funny. The trainees thought it was terrifying. He and his roommates eventually decided to prank the instructors back with candy bars, pornos, and Tupac music. When they began regretting their plan as the instructors came closer, they were surprised when one of them raised the music volume and ordered them to dance. The others took the bait as they spent the next moments eating the candy, flipping the magazines, and laughing as the trainees danced. They congratulated them for passing the inspection. It was a huge success. But the worst had yet to come.

Pool-training exercises were harder. Some SEALs had even died during them, especially during the "beehive" where a hundred and seventy recruits fought to stay afloat in a deep, crowded pool. Rob would survive by swimming to the bottom, finding the edge from below, and swimming to back to the surface. The one-length sprint eventually caught him because of his major disadvantage from the collegiate swimmers and the instructors pranking him into wearing a shirt because of his sunburn. He eventually won the race after asking permission from Instructor Joe Hawes to take the shirt off.

To survive BUD/S, one had to commit himself. His only priority should only be BUD/S. Every day was like torture in those two weeks. In their lives, there was only BUD/s. It sounded like hell but Hell had not even begun yet.

Chapter Four

On a Sunday before Hell Week, while everyone tried – and failed - to sleep inside their tents, Rob's new know-it-all swim buddy broke down. Rob tried to calm him down but Hell Week began to start with its infamous deafening explosions and unloaded weapons fired into the night while instructors screamed into the tents with conflicting orders. During this mayhem, everyone was desperately trying to stay with their swim buddies. The hours-long, panic-filled drill was made to see how the trainees handle stress without knowing what was going on. Among the confusion, screaming, and berating instructors, some started to quit right then. With those quitters was Rob's new swim buddy.

Those who were left managed to organize their boat crews and paddle towards the surf zone a mile north of waterfront of Hotel del Coronado. Rob and his team had no chance to think or reflect because the huge waves sent their boat closer and closer to the rocks. Luckily, their lead men managed to recover from a fall and their group successfully heaved their boat over the rocks. Their relief was short-lived as they were ordered to do it again. And again. More men began to quit.

Hell Week was very similar to the regular BUD/S training of the past weeks, except that they were required to do it while carrying a 320-pound rubber raft everywhere, even the obstacle courses, with the obvious exception of the cargo net and the slide for life. Soon, the trainees started to despise hearing "UP-BOAT". They would lift the rafts and rest it on their heads as weight was added or as instructors themselves stand on the boat. Eventually, everyone would fail and drop the boat. Rob understood that the SEAL instructors were searching for men who don't blame others for not carrying the weight, the men who, no matter what, worked together as a team.

As one of the shortest guys, Rob was grouped with Crew II, mostly known as the Smurf Crew, who always come up last in all races and get extra unpleasant attention from the instructors. More so during Elephant Walks where they can't keep up with the other boats in a single-file line as they jogged around California.

The trainees grew increasingly tired and started to get shin splints from overstressed ligaments. Rob managed to handle his by stretching his hamstring but the others couldn't deal with it and started to quit, joining the increasing population of "the quitter line." Some held on to petroleum jelly that the doctors give during their checkups. A handful was not enough for the full-body chafing so it went to their more delicate parts instead. All the time, they were cold and exhausted and hurting. Rob met one of his best friends, Sterling, after he followed Rob's request to pee on his freezing hands.

The instructors used the cold to hunt out quitters. At the Steel Pier, the trainees were required to strip off their clothes and perform life-saving drills in the water for a few minutes. It would be followed by treading the water for thirty minutes. Then, the shivering men would lie down on the frigid steel pier as the instructors sprayed them with hoses. They would even offer dry clothes, warm food, and even coffee if they would just quit. It was no wonder that most quitters from Class 208 came from the merciless steel pier.

One of the Hell Week victims was Rob's friend John who even avoided him so Rob couldn't talk him out of it. That Wednesday morning though, the instructors seemed to ease up on them as if surviving sixty hours of brutal physical punishment without sleep was the true key in being accepted in the SEAL. On the last night of Hell Week, a Thursday night, it was Class 208's turn to do "Around the World" and race their boats around the island. However, since the admiral was late to officially bring Hell Week to an end, the instructors ordered the survivors to leave their boats and plunge into a horrible sewage mud pit. The admiral finally showed up at noon, gave a speech, and shook each of their filthy hands.

At last, Hell Week was finished and the survivors received their first rite of passage: a brown shirt replacing their whites and greens. Rob's parents, with the help of Instructor A, would help them sneak into medical and surprise him. Rob, thinking that his parents were just from his imagination, dismissed them. After the medical exam, he was given an entire tube of petroleum jelly, a Gatorade, and a large pizza. It turned out that two of his three roommates made it and they celebrated their first proper sleep. Ten hours later, Rob woke up to find a note that informed him that his parents were actually waiting for him to take Rob for breakfast. It wasn't his imagination after all.

Chapter Five

The Walk Week followed Hell Week, which was the only free week of Phase Two they were given to recover. After that was the usual evolutions during the day and hydrographic reconnaissance and WWII-era Underwater Demolition Team (UDT) tactics lessons during the night. As instructors tortured their brains with primitive eighteenth-century technology that they would never use; they also made sure that their bodies had a similar treatment through timed ocean swims. Still, it was their first time hearing instructors encouragingly say that they would make it as SEALs since they survived Hell Week.

Normally, diving would have been an exhilarating experience. But at BUD/S, the trainees were required to understand diving physics and diving medicine to avoid exploding lungs or arterial gas embolism due to pressure changes on the way up. Flunking the infamous written tests was no option: it would get them rolled back into the next class and start the PTRR and Hell Week again.

After surviving the test, the trainees would face the Pool Week which required them to run to the pool more than a mile from the compound while carrying old school sixty-pound SCUBA "twin 80s" tanks. They also had their scuba gear rigged so the instructors could see how they dealt with drowning panic. The Pool Competency Test was another excuse to scare them in diving near surf zones.

Rob's class took the test on Friday; they were alphabetically called one at a time to the pool. Without seeing what was going on with the preceding trainees, Rob could only hear "I FEEL FINE!" from the surfacing men, the safety sentence that ensured that one could pronounce "f" and thus, did not experience embolism. Despite them saying the words correctly, the instructors would declare them as failed. Finally, it was Rob's time. As he swam, his masks and fins were removed roughly and his air was turned off. He waited for the "simulation" to end before turning his air back on and crawling on the pool floor. The instructors continued to occasionally knot his air hoses and hit him hard. On his fifth hit, the instructor tied a "whammy knot" which was impossible to undo. Although Rob held his breath for a minute and tried his best, he was forced to resurface and shout "I FEEL FINE!" Like the others before him, he failed the test. By the end of the day, only half the class had passed.

Knowing that he only had two chances left, Rob used the rest of the weekend to practice nonstop until sunset. During his second try, he finally achieved a pass after he managed to unknot three of the instructor's whammy knots. Sadly, Dave, his boat crew's motivational leader and one of the people who made Rob kept going, failed for the fourth time.

Eventually though, Dave would graduate with Class 209 and would join the West Coast SEAL teams.

During their actual dive training, Rob found himself enjoying the real Navy SEAL stuff of diving underneath ships and propellers to locate mine targets and welding seams. Rob even managed to save his class from physical training after shooting a three-pointer on his knees from an instructor's dare. It didn't save them from the 5.5-nautical-mile swim against the current, specifically sabotaged by their instructors. After five and a half hours swimming with his original swim buddy Monte, they saw a big commotion of instructors and the executive officer yelling for them to get out of the water as they neared the surf zone. They later learned that the XO found out about the instructors' dangerous plans that would have put them in very life-threatening situations. Rob was satisfied knowing that the mean instructors would get an earful from their boss. But, he had a weekend to enjoy with his buddies.

The next morning, the instructors were back with revenge as they made the trainees redo the 5.5 mile swim hallway to the Imperial Beach and back. They were so pissed that Rob and Monte smuggled a Snickers Bar just to make their swim a little less miserable. Thankfully, all of the survivors passed this time.

19

Chapter Six

The Phase Three of the BUD/S actually had its fun parts because of the Naval shooting ranges in San Diego and multiday "camping" trips at Mount Laguna for land navigation. The fun stopped at San Clemente Island.

After a lesson for "shark appreciation," they would conduct a "shark appreciation swim" at night. In their next few weeks though, the trainees practiced the old-school frogman style of blowing up WWII obstacles underwater. For forty days and forty nights, they moved on to weapons and small unit tactics. It did sound fun only until the instructors got bored and made them their source of entertainment.

Rob's new swim buddy and roommate, Parker, began to break down after having to leave his girlfriend in San Diego. Because the instructors liked him, they merely punished him even if he kept messing up. Rob, unfortunately, as his swim buddy, had to join Parker during punishments. Luckily, when the SEAL Team Three messed up during their drills, Class 208's dive training was temporarily canceled for the next days. When Parker screwed up again while diving was still prohibited, Rob volunteered to spray him with the hose every hour instead. Eventually, Parker was rolled back like Dave and graduated with Class 209.

With the next forty days swimming, learning, and blowing stuff up, their bodies started to heal and build up. Rob surprised himself after seeing his "Pillsbury Doughboy" mid-section with a six-pack abs. They were handed "Dream Sheets" a few weeks before the BUD/S training finale so they could fill in their top three choices for team assignment. Rob blindly chose Team Two, the oldest and the richest in history, so he could use his combat training. Fortunately, Rob was chosen by his dream team. He still had the photograph of him and his buddy Monte who went to SEAL Team One.

The following Friday, thirty-three survivors from Class 208's two hundred waited for their names to be called by their beloved Instructor A. Rob would never forget how Instructor A called a hundred and seventy names and revealed that those were the quitters while the rest of the men standing were the "BUD/S Studs."

Nobody could predict who would make it through the BUD/S. Not the boot camp instructors who tried to prepare promising rookies by special workouts and training. Not the psychologists that the brass brought in. Eighty percent always don't make it. It wasn't about the race, or size, musculature, or I.Q. In the end, it was sheer determination and strength of the mind.

After his graduation, Rob celebrated with his family and later attended Basic Airborne school at Fort Benning, Georgia before reporting to SEAL Team Two. Unlike BUD/S, the jumping class instructors were really nice to the cocky graduates. Rob was so enthusiastic in jumping even though it took almost three weeks for him to master the landing. All of his Class 208 brothers graduated on time with their silver wing pin. Still, Rob wanted to get the infamous rite of passage "blood wings" so he had his instructors punch his pins into his chest.

Now it was time to check in with the legendary SEAL Team Two.

Chapter Seven

Of course Rob had to risk his SEAL team position by drinking a beer on the sidewalk as an under-aged guy. If it weren't for his brother's expired license and luck, he wouldn't have made it to the Naval Amphibious Base, much less join the SEALs if the cop arrested him on alcohol-related charge.

Rob managed to check in on Friday so he could orient themselves. With their meager paychecks, Rob just shared a Navy barracks room with his friend from Class 208, Christian, and ate at the Navy galley. With the real SEALs deal, all signs of cockiness fell away.

And of course he was assigned to the legendary and intimidating Instructor Woodie who sent uncountable recruits quitting. At first Rob thought he was a prick but Rob would find out that Woodie would be one of the nicest, big-hearted guys he ever knew. There was also equality between the SEAL officers and the enlisted; first names were used and salutes weren't required all the time. Neil Roberts, the holder of the "O" course record at BUD/S, impressed Rob greatly because of his efficiency, purpose, and generosity: everything that Rob aspired to be.

It also turned out that the SEALs were rarely sent in covert ops and never really had several kills back in 1997. Their last real action was the invasion of Panama in 1989 by SEAL Team Four. After that, there were some fights in Somalia and peripheral involvement in the first Gulf War but otherwise, there was no other significant operation. Their "can't talk about it" replies to civilians merely gave them the impression of untold secret missions which never really happened.

To become actual SEALs though, Rob and the rookies had to undergo additional tactical training for thirteen weeks. Since the classes only occur a couple of times a year, they would spend their days working out and learning to match the SEALs great humor. They welcomed the SEAL tradition of hiding from the Tuesday ocean swimming and the good-natured hazing of talking trash while interrupting the newbies as they introduce themselves.

After the command deemed that they were ready, Rob underwent the intense two-hour oral exam. To beat the "all-around super SEAL" Art, he decided to cheat by skipping some tires in the "O" course. A new guy, Mark, called him out but Rob merely called him an asshole. Rob was in it for a surprise to see that his review panel for the test was actually Mark. The guy paid him back by grilling him on the test. Fortunately, Rob got his Trident pin and was now officially a Naval Special Warfare Operator.

Chapter Eight

It was almost two years before Rob got his first nautical deployment by boarding the USS *Austin* at Camp Lejeune to Rota, Spain as a part of the Mobile Amphibious Ready Group. It was also his first experience around Marines who impressed him because of their superior sniping skills. Their sniper course in the Naval Special Warfare was designed by the history-famous Gunnery Sergeant Carlos Hathcock, a marine who had ninety-three confirmed kills in Vietnam and had took out an enemy sniper by a bullet passing through his telescopic scope to the eye. Hathcock's successors aboard USS *Austin* were worthy and Rob found himself having sniper bonding activities with them.

Rob quickly grew accustomed to the constant sway of the ship and even liked it. He respected the people aboard the ship, doing jobs harder than the SEALS in the dark with the heat of machines but without receiving any recognition. Meanwhile, the SEALS aboard the ships would just "Sleep, Eat, and Lift", play cards, and get to know each other. To get out of the cabin fever, they would swim two miles into the Atlantic Ocean. Rob dared himself to smoke a cigarette in the middle of the ocean – that was one of his firsts too.

Their voyage was also Rob's first tour of Europe which was a real eye-opener for him. Without a war, their only missions were prearranged exercises with various North Atlantic

Treaty Organization (NATO) allies. During one of their barrel-shooting practices aboard a helicopter in Huey, their engine suddenly exploded. Their Marine pilot flicked his cigarette out of the window and maneuvered the falling chopper towards the ship to hit the stern and skid forward. They were unhurt and the Navy mechanics even managed to rebuild the helicopter.

That was Rob's first helicopter engine explosion before the second, which happened the following week in Italy aboard an H-53 for their exercises. Its engine blew on takeoff and the pilots impressively softened their crash by autorotation, saving the crew just in time to watch their most awaited movie: *Saving Private Ryan*.

Finally, Rob got his first real action in Tirana, Albania after a plot to attack senior officials in the embassy was uncovered by the intelligence. Rob could remember someone mentioning the name of Osama bin Laden. As he and his friend Mike Johnson went on patrol wearing their plainclothes, some kids drove by and fired automatic weapons to make noise. It was his first time to be fired on but they couldn't catch up with their car. In the end of their deployment, Rob was assigned to a sniper position while the president of Albania met with some admirals. Much to his disappointment, there was no action and he merely got sunburn.

It was in the early 2000s that Rob would get his first deployment to the Middle East aboard an aircraft carrier. Their mission would make the headlines worldwide as Rob and nine other SEALs recovered documents aboard the Russian commercial oil tanker *Volganeft* proving that they smuggled Iraqi oil, a violation of the United Nations sanctions. It was his first helicopter-borne vessel boarding and one of his first experiences with interrogations.

The next year, they were deployed to Kosovo to continue the peacekeeping in Germany and conduct reconnaissance and surveillance. That included hiding in the mountains to observe the locals and walking through minefields. They learned two things: Covert R&S teams get compromised by unassuming locals most of the time and that plugging ears through the minefields is useless.

Rob and his team went back to their barracks in the late summer. As they watched the television, they witnessed the news reports about a passenger jet slicing the first tower of the World Trade Center in New York, going out in a massive fireball which was still billowing smoke. That moment changed their lives, among the others'.

Rob never really expected a long SEAL career but he knew the desperation of the moment and he was excited to actually put his training to use and serve his country. They returned from Germany and by March 4, 2002, they geared up for a

27

deployment in the Mediterranean. As he packed his parachutes at Little Creek, Rob was informed of Neil Robert's death. This man who had impressed Rob greatly participated in the Operation Anaconda to establish an observation point. An error about the al-Qaeda and Taliban numbers and a helicopter malfunction exposed them to the anti-aircraft guns. As seen from a drone feed, Roberts managed to survive his fall and held off a swarm of terrorists without his rifle until he went down. His teammates attempted a rescue but also took causalities. Eventually, reinforcements and air support aided to fight the seventeen-hour battle to take the summit observation point at the cost of six American lives. To honor the brave SEAL, they mounted his broken weapon which proved that Roberts went down fighting with only his pistol, grenades, and knife. Aside from his gun and his bullet-holed helmet, they recovered Roberts' letter for his wife with his words: "Although I sacrificed personal freedom and many other things, I got just as much as I gave. My time in the Teams was special. For all the times I was cold, wet, tired, sore, scared, hungry and angry, I had a blast."

When his death reached Rob that day, war finally became real.

Chapter Nine

To participate in the fight against bin Laden, Rob tried out for SEAL Team X (blotted for confidentiality). He waited a year for the results as he continued his training and deployment with his current team. He also helped his sister Kelly move to Virginia Beach who, in return, helped him hook up with a young blonde named Nicole. Rob pursued her for a long time and finally got married about a year and a half later. He also made it through the Team X screening and was sent to Arizona.

There, the SEALs practiced the dangerous high-Altitude, low-opening (HALO) and high-altitude, high-opening (HAHO) skydiving. Rob almost plummeted to the ground after testing a faster high-performance parachute. He was lucky enough to get freed from the cords and knew that he and his friends ought to report the system. They didn't however, and it would later haunt Rob in a cruel way.

The next training involved a close quarters battle (CQB) which was the most famous and most difficult. It would include a fast breaching of cramped buildings with hostile armed enemies and civilians. The instructors would ingrain the awareness and safety violations as they practiced thousands of times. On one of their last runs, Rob's buddy almost shot him because of pressure. His mistake sent him on a plane that afternoon and Rob never saw him again. It was very important to understand in CQB that communication is the key and that there is no time to think slow nor cave in to pressure.

The next training was in Washington State's Survival, Evasion, Resistance, and Escape school. It was a war game exercise where instructors were allowed to beat up men to simulate arrest, interrogation, and torture in a foreign role-play. Afterwards, they were taught of what they were supposed to say by layering stories and straight lies.

Rob was sent home after his officers learned that his wife was in labor. With a new daughter and required workouts and trainings, it almost felt like Hell Week again. Nicole was not worried about Rob though since she joined a support group for SEAL wives. Dying in combat was also rare back then.

He successfully completed training by December 2004 with the thirty-four other completers out of the starting sixty. Rob was chosen by his preferred combat hardened squadron responsible for Operation Anaconda and ambush for Roberts' supposed rescue. Despite him being a new father and a husband, he wanted to avenge Robert's and the others' deaths. When he entered the "Team Room" for the first time,

Rob was in awe as he saw the memorabilia all over the walls and met these hardened and experienced men. He would also learn about what to expect and how to let the Navy grooming standards go.

Their squadron was also a team of pranksters who excelled in creativity and denial. Stink bombs, pink-dyeing uniforms, and applying "liquid heat" lotions in the groin parts of trousers: it was all a part of life. Rob's locker row was known as "The Gaza Strip" because of exploding pranks. It was no wonder that morale and camaraderie was high. They also had the "Yard-In Party" tradition before deployment, where one must drink non-stop from a yard-long glass tube filled with ice cold beer and whiskey.

At the end of the yarding, their Command Master Chief awarded Rob and his best friends with their patches. Rob felt honored and pride to finish nine years of the most difficult training imaginable and become part of the team. Finally, he was going to war.

Chapter Ten

Rob's daughter was not even a year old when he had to kiss he goodbye for his first combat mission. They flew aboard a C-17 cargo plane on April 2005 to hunt high-value al-Qaeda targets in Afghanistan. His next flight, this time on a C-130 prop plane, flew him to their Jalalabad safe house with two other SEALs, an Explosive Ordnance Disposal (EOD) guy, and a radio operator. Rob met his first Afghan who they called Larry who served as their interpreter on Rob's first truck ride. Not knowing if he could trust Larry, Rob was curt and cautious around him. The same went for Jalalabad, a city where Osama bin Laden used to live.

His team leader and master breacher, Adam, greeted them in the safe house. Rob was thrilled to be working together with a Team X legend who was awarded with a Silver Star after hiking through the snow and defeating al-Qaeda terrorists and their anti-helicopter machine guns during Operation Anaconda. After briefing the SEALs, Adam gave a tour of the Chocolate Alley and the neighborhood. While waiting for mission clearance, Rob and his team spent their time eating, lifting, watching, and going shopping in the bazaars. Their time wasn't all wasted with idle activities as they interviewed potential guards, electricians, and interpreters from the locals while wearing their casuals to blend in. Children occasionally come out and beg for chocolates, hence the name of the street, and started to love the chocolate-rich Americans. The Americans loved them back.

Their first mission in Afghanistan was to track down hostiles in their own neighborhood using new technologies. They blew the Saudi Arabian suspect's front gate and rolled in just like in their CQB training. Of course, there were multiple civilians inside but with the help of the interpreters and candy, the SEALs managed to roll them up. Rob cuffed the Arab while laughing at his funny shirt. The low-level terrorist was flown to Bagram. The expert interrogators would handle the rest.

There was no need to be stressed during operations. Rob learned to do them just like the way he practiced a million times. Sure enough, a dozen more missions followed without a single shot fired from both sides. Their team leader, Adam, was equally calm, a trait that would prove itself essential when they almost shot Afghan cops on patrol during an operation.

By June 2005, the command sent some men from SEAL Team Ten and SEAL Delivery Vehicle Team One. Apparently, they wanted to put up snipers in the Korengal "Valley of Death" to eliminate Taliban and al-Qaeda warlords, specifically Ahmad Shah. The team leaders and SEAL Team

Ten commander Erik Kristensen, who was also a task unit commander, convened for the attack plan. The top brass did not recommend the incursion because of the terrorists' surface-to-air missiles.

A recon team of SEAL Delivery Vehicle snipers were sent to the valley while Team Ten flew to Jalalabad to meet up with Team X and prepare their attack. Rob was reunited with his sniper school friend Mike Healy. Team X was envious at first since Team Ten was going to see some significant action. The outstation chief denied their requests though and tried to convince SEAL Team Ten to back out.

Little did Team X knew as they swam in their tiny pool, the four SEAL snipers had been spotted and fifty enemies began a catastrophic three-sided attack. Although they managed to escape down the slope, all were wounded and the location made it impossible to send a distress call. Dietz, the communications guy, was shot through the hand when he tried to emerge from cover. Murphy had no choice but to use his satellite phone to contact SOF Quick Reaction Force as he sprinted to an open field. Shot in the back, he still managed to complete the call while firing at the enemy until he could return to cover.

Some helicopters took off immediately for rescue. One

Chinook chopper, dubbed "Turbine 33" with eight SEALs and eight other men on board, left behind the other slower helicopters to reach their snipers in time. Without the cover of night, the chopper was shot down with their leader, Kristensen. Only Mike Healy survived since he switched out to another helicopter before take-off.

The shaken pilots landed on the wrong base and returned to Jalalabad airfield. According to the survivors, Turbine 33 was targeted by heat-seeking missiles which narrowly missed Turbine 34. With no rescue and their situations unknown, the SEAL snipers ran out of ammunition after keeping enemies at bay for two hours and killing a few dozen. Outnumbered and outgunned, Murphy, Axelson, and Dietz died but Luttrell miraculously survived – albeit injured badly – by crawling away from Korengal Valley for a day. Locals eventually aided him in a nearby village.

With the anti-aircraft missile defenses, there was no choice but to ask for any Special Forces volunteers: Army Rangers, Air Force men, Navy, EOD, SEALs, and Green Berets. They hiked for ten hours through the steep dirt mountains as heat and dehydration caught up with them.

Meanwhile, Karen, whose husband Jeff was killed in the Turbine 33 explosion, received the horrible news. Nicole,

35

who was equally anxious, tried to console her until baby duties forced her to return home. When she saw Rob's neighbor, Ron, wearing his uniform and knocking her door, Nicole almost fainted. In reality, Ron only knocked because she dropped a bib full of baby poo so the distressed Nicole punched him for giving her the frights.

As command, who were still oblivious to the snipers' fate, started to fly some men to secure the crash site and recover the bodies, Rob and the others were informed that Axelson was MIA, possibly dead. The hiking volunteers continued at night and saw Taliban men around a fire. They called in an air strike, which was one of the coolest things Rob ever saw: A-10s screaming, flying low, and sending supersonic Gatling bullets overhead. The volunteers finally reached the bottom and drove their trucks to search for the MIA snipers. They still haven't slept for two days.

Following their Afghan code of Pashtunwali: the obligation to protect strangers entering their homes, the villagers refused to give up Luttrell to the Taliban (Ironically, it was the same code that prevented their leader Mullah Mohammed Omar to hand over Osama bin Laden). A village elder carried Luttrell's note and showed the Americans his location. Command refused a rescue since they believe it was a trap but the volunteers were determined to bring their soldier back. They met with some Marines on the way as the old man practically "flew" up the mountain to guide them.

The volunteers didn't let dehydration and lack of sleep stop them until they reached the hilltop. A helicopter managed to extract Luttrell as the tired Americans sleepwalked and sleep-drived to the base, where they slept for twenty-five hours.

Chapter Eleven

It was late 2005 back in Virginia Beach when Rob received news that the Army Special Forces in western Iraq were receiving huge attacks and lost an entire troop. When Team X announced that they would join the fight in Iraq, Rob was excited even though it was a more dangerous than Afghanistan with suicide bombings everywhere. Al-Qaeda had studied their tactics and would trap or ambush the Americans with their own counterattack. But Team X was determined to change the old tactic traditions and make up their own.

Team X flew to Al Asad Air Base on January 2006. They made the abandoned building their new screen-and-equipment-filled homestead. Rob also bonded with their team's rookies. Jonny Savio, who Rob had bought a beer before after the smart rescue swimmer impressed him for finishing his own Hell Week as first in his class, would become one of his best friends in the years ahead. The other guy was Andy, a transfer from the British Special Boat Service who survived the 2003 invasion of Iraq.

Their missions were like clockwork. The intelligence would conduct surveillance and investigation until they could identify a target, they would brief the strike team until they accepted, the strike team would prepare their gear, command would form a plan, combat dogs would be chosen, and the team would launch. They steadily worked from the bottom of the terrorist pyramid to reach the No.1 target, the bombing and massacre mastermind: Abu Musab al-Zarqawi.

Sure enough, Team X's slower but more methodical version of using night vision to stay invisible and surprise enemies was showing its effectiveness. With almost their every night spent doing missions, the assault team worked on tactics and started to learn new things while their paired-up sniper, Greg, piled up his kills. Rob would joke that snipers kill more people but the assaulters kill more famous people. They still haven't killed any famous one. Yet.

In one particular mission to hit three major compounds controlled by terrorists, Team X showcased their new tactics. However, as Rob and the SEALs methodically made their way to the target in stealth, the Army Special Forces and the British flew ahead on loud choppers, announcing their arrival. The SEALs were forced to hasten but still followed their dark tactics. They were like ghosts as they quietly breached Building 1-1, their target, to the point that terrorists in front of them could not even see them. It was also Andy's first kill.

But there was no room for fear or surprise. Rob's team

finished clearing the house as the snipers went hot outside. Jonny and Rob left the building, saw that their sniper Dirty was covering for them, and made their move. Hundred hours of practice made the pair perfectly in sequence as they shot two enemies that popped out the alley. Those were their first kills. They continued taking the building, even saving a weaponless and injured al-Qaeda along the way. Rob was thankful for the poorly-shot bullets and the enemy's belief that Allah would guide their shots. He wouldn't have been standing today if not for those.

Eventually, the mujahideen retreated to a nearby mosque to make their last stand. Since the snipers were blocked by the mosque doors, Team X called in the Rangers with their Carl Gustav rocket launchers and sent three of them blasting through the mosque. When Rob and his team arrived later, he would be haunted, not by the gruesome sight of shredded broken bodies, but by the sound of blood flowing from a severed arm.

As they did the debrief, the thought of his first kill finally settled in Rob's mind. He felt no remorse for the man who dedicated his life destroying Western culture and celebrated after bombing a tourist hotel full of men, women, and children. There was no remorse for their cult of death.

Chapter Twelve

By 2006, Rob had a house, a mortgage, a wife, and kids. But with his 325 days each year away from home as a Navy SEAL, his family had to make large sacrifices, haunted by the threat of the war and of his permanent absence. On the autumn of 2006 in Afghanistan, he almost did.

It was an operation at night on a large maze-like compound. On this particular mission, Rob had his friend Lance, still known for his infamous "good yard gone bad" patching ceremony by drinking his own puke on his yarding, was now famous again because of his death-defying incidents of near-misses. One particular incident was in Iraq in 2005, where Lance fell into a swimming pool, almost drowned because of the weight of his gear, and almost got electrocuted from a live power line hanging down to touch the water. Another time, in Arizona, Lance almost killed himself and their super sniper Greg by jumping too early.

As the pair swept the area, they finally reached a corner room where Rob had to take the risk and clear the room full of blindspots. Luckily, thirty meters away in the dark, the same super sniper spotted an enemy in Rob's blindspot and took care of it before Rob was attacked. Rob was impressed by the fact that Greg could recognize him by his gait. Later, Greg would also save Lance from getting attacked by a house pet.

There were also other aggressive guys like Nate, an excellent SEAL, who wanted to get kills but got none. During one of their missions in Iraq, they sent Toby the dog to hunt down mujahideen hiding in palm groves away from their safe houses. The "fur missile" immediately darted off to bite an enemy as soon as the Belgian Malinois caught the scent. The panicking terrorist almost shot the poor dog if Nate had not shot him in the head first. Nate finally got his first kill.

Rob and his team would experience a lot during their deployment. They would learn how to evolve from the equally adapting al-Qaeda terrorists until they became the most lethal and stealthy team in modern history.

Chapter Thirteen

It was always strange to come home from war to a routine of training exercises. Rob found himself miserably packing, unpacking, and repacking four-hundred-square-foot of parachutes the whole day in the spring of 2007 until Nicole called him and told him she was pregnant. Babies were one of the best expensive and stress-inducing things to happen in his life. But, Rob had to go back to the war in the summer.

Back in Iraq, the tide of the war had shifted. General David Petraeus, the top American commander in the area, had persuaded the Sunni Muslims of the Anbar Province to turn against the al-Qaeda. The incident was known as "The Anbar Awakening." By May of 2007, the number of SEALs and American soldiers in Iraq were growing as the numbers of terrorists were decreasing. More SEALs were accepted through the BUD/S and sent to Afghanistan. Rob's troop commander Rich, the highest-ranked SEAL in Iraq, chose his skeleton crew to go under the radar.

Rob found himself back in the Anbar Province where his team installed themselves in a former mansion near the Tigris River. They went out pretty much every night to hunt targets. To minimize their time in one of their missions, Rob built a rolling seven-foot adhesive strip of C-6 plastic explosive.

When set, it would make a thunderous noise. The charge did just that when Rob set it off on building 1-1, their primary target. It sent a woman combatant near the door to the ceiling. Killing a woman, even as an enemy, made Rob guilty. But there was no time to indulge in that. Rob and his team mate, Delicious, finished clearing up the rooms, their invisibility in the dark and their night vision proving effective against insurgents. However, Rob would later discover that they just orphaned three children, children the same age as their own kids. He felt terrible so he escorted the children to their aunt, despite it being reckless. Rob would never forget how their aunt waved at him as she brought the kids inside.

When Rob returned to the fight, there were gunshots all around them. It was not surprising, being in the heart of al-Qaeda territory and the heavy resistance. They eventually met up with the second team leader, Street, who cleared the secondary target. They rolled up all the arrested men and left the women and children behind, ensuring that the rest of the American fighters would not mistake them for enemies. They eliminated seven al-Qaeda terrorists that night and took nine more to their base. From all the missions that they experienced, it wasn't even considered unusually eventful.

Rob and his team reached the peak of their stealth skills to the point that they played "counting coup" games, in honor of the Native American warriors. They would silently breach rooms by lock picking or window removal, creep to the sleeping terrorists, check for suicide vests, and wake them up until they cried or poop their pants.

Eventually, their several successful missions seriously thinned the al-Qaeda population in Ramadi. Commander Rich, as a considerably humble SEAL, believed that working under the Army Special Forces in Baghdad would benefit his men and the overall operation. SEAL Team X was flown to Baghdad International Airport, which, being in the heart of American military, was impressive with its cargo planes, jets, bombers, and attack planes. To build up their own homestead, Team X had to steal amenities from the "Fobbits," who hogged all of the good stuff, and salvage from the Navy's Construction Battalion or Seabees. His mate, Cole, nicknamed Boots from his boot-shopping fiasco that made him late at BUD/S training and running alone inside a house full of enemies to "deliver the boots", took care of the salvaged pieces and built their furniture. Soon, they had weird furniture that smelled like dumpsters, a nice gym, and coffeemakers.

Chapter Fourteen

Right from the start, SEAL Team X was glad to work with the Army Special Forces because of their exciting and fun style of attack. When Team X, codenamed Task Force Blue, were chosen by the Joint Operations Center (JOC) to rush a terrorist cell and take one alive, the bored SEALs decided to fly and land directly in front of the house. Their plan was overconfident though, since they were so used in being right and stop thinking that things could go wrong. That was how success could kill.

As expected, the enemy were ready and opened fire while they were still on the chopper. The helicopters managed to hit the deck at the same time as the SEALs jumped out with the cover of darkness. They eliminated three of the fighters quickly as the rest spread out. Echo Team took care of the house on the right as Rob and Delta Team took the left. They tried calling out the terrorists instead of rushing in with blazing guns. With no replies, they let loose Toby the fearless dog. Toby, with his keen sense of smell, located the insurgent hiding in a dugout beneath the bathtub. Luckily, the SEALs managed to kill him before he blew himself up with the Americans.

Dogs had been an essential part of their operation especially in chasing down escapees or locating their hideouts. These fierce and magnificent creatures were so far from the mangy scavengers they see in the streets. In fear, they would try to shoot one whenever they could. Back in the base, the SEALs would play with the dogs but were careful to keep the dominance in check. Rob and his mates have seen a few dogs die in combat and would mourn them like one of their brothers. There is a wall memorial for their fallen dogs in front of the SEAL Team X headquarters in Virginia, a few feet ahead and a right from the black wall with the names of the fallen soldiers. Because that was where the dogs walked: forward and to the right of their humans.

On the other hand, Rob was enjoying the full vehicle arsenal of Baghdad. One such day, while hunting for a target, Rob and his team used the lightly armored, highly maneuverable, small and quiet Pandurs to chase him around the city. However, their target managed to escape through a bridge. Worrying that the bridge was wired to explode, their troop commander Rich called off the chase, much to the team's disappointment. Rob knew that it was the right call and explained to the rest of his mates that they should not let emotion cloud their judgement in crucial decisions.

Because terrorists started to move out, Team X decided to do the same by heading to Baqubah. Their air-conditioned tents became their new home as they waited for their first mission: Improvised Explosive Device (IED) producers on a small peninsula. Rob understood the importance of taking out these producers since they were responsible for the majority of American casualties. But, the peninsula was in a good position: too many civilians for an airstrike, a risky size for a chopper, and only one road which was littered with IEDs. They had one choice: swim in.

Seventeen SEALs, two combat dogs, and a few enablers crept up the swamp and swam for about two hours until they reached dry land. Their plan in camping up snipers and entering the buildings with stealth was quickly compromised when a sentry spotted them and started shooting. Miraculously, the shots missed them all and the SEALs adjusted to find cover. Their super sniper Greg did his job and rained death on the terrorists from the rooftop. With the rest of the fighters fully aware of the ruckus, the assault team rushed to the main entry in the cover of darkness. While D team swept the buildings and watched over the women and children, E and F teams eliminated the others they encountered and the ones trying to escape. The mission was perfectly successful: all nineteen terrorists were dead without causing injury from any woman or child without taking any casualties.

With their oppressors dead, the peninsula held a huge party that attracted the newspaper reporters in Baghdad. When the reporter asked a woman on who came that night, she responded: "Ninjas, and they came with lions." That was the headline the next day in Baghdad.

Chapter Fifteen

Back from war, back to parachutes. On this particular jump, Rob had Lance as the jumpmaster so it was not surprising that something "interesting" was about to happen. While jumping a HAHO without goggles, Rob found himself jumping right above a storm and getting himself hit by hail. The next day, it was a young Air Force para-rescue guy who got unlucky after his cord wrapped over the top of his parachute. Greg managed to notice the anomaly and told him to cut off the cord and open his reserve. The jumping team got lucky when a commercial passenger jet flew so close past them that Rob could see the pilot's US Airways insignia. Obviously, somebody didn't pay any attention to the passing aircraft report.

In late winter of 2008, before they got another deployment to Afghanistan, Lance decided to take one of the most dangerous jump-training courses in Arizona. Everyone decided against it because of his incredible bad luck. Rob was supposed to go with him but he was sent to a mission to rescue some hostages in Colombia. When Rob finished his own jump and packed up his parachute, his boss, Street, approached him and told him that Lance died.

Rob could recall something like an electric shock when he

heard that one of his brothers had died. They had lost Tom Valentine in another parachute malfunction, Mike Koch and Nate Hardy were killed while clearing a compound in Iraq, and Mark Carter stepped on an IED.

And now it was Lance. What was more horrifying was the fact that he had died with a similar parachute problem that almost killed Rob a year earlier. If only Rob had reported it a year before, maybe Lance was still alive. Before Team X had started losing so many guys, command had ordered them to fill out "What I want if I die" sheets which they merely treated as a joke.

To honor Lance who would have been happy if they pulled off his "if I die" wishes, the remaining Team X decided to do his: Lance's body being buried in a Pennsylvanian cemetery, a Camaro to pull up the gravesite and play music from his favorite band at top volume while they stood around drinking Natural Light, his mom placing the first shovelful of dirt on his coffin to be followed by his mates, and finally, for Team X to visit a porno bar right down the street.

Chapter Sixteen

Rob's eyes were opened to the different perspectives of the Afghan locals during his stay in a former Russian military base in Asadabad. Many locals, especially in the remote regions, still had primitive beliefs such as dragons and the moon only being an inch big.

At that point in the war, they were working with an elite, well-trained, and well-paid Afghani team, which Rob was a bit worried about because of their priorities. That was also his first deployment as a team leader, more specifically, a chief petty officer. They were assigned with a worthy target: Zabit Jalil, the perpetrator of the "lone survivor" ambush on a SEAL recon team, killing three and shooting down a rescue helicopter.

They decided to do a bait-and-switch operation and a tactic that would allow them to chase the enemy even if they slipped to the Pakistani border. Hopefully, Jalil's people would spot them and attack while Rob would call in artillery and air support until they retreated.

As team leader, Rob would serve as the Ground Force Commander directing the action. He ordered the gear to be split up because of the long hike in steep slopes. He also took Tom and Seth from the US Army, their interpreter for transmissions, and forty Afghans aboard a CH-47. Rob organized a fallback position just in case they needed to fight down the hill with twenty-five Afghans and their mortars. He also split up the team into two flanks to make themselves look outmanned. Alone and with no observing planes to create unnecessary noise, Rob and his team waited.

When the sun came up, they began to see activity on the Pakistan side of the border: six armed men around a few tents in what seemed to be a checkpoint. It was clear that they had noticed Rob and his men and were discussing what to do. Later, four of them began walking to their right flank and yelled. The interpreter informed him that they were calling for the senior officer to come down for tea. As planned, Rob had their own Afghans to tell the men that they were part of the Afghan patrols and that there were no Americans.

After tea, the Afghans returned and informed that the men were the "Frontier Corps" hired by the US to guard the Afghan/Pakistan border. Rob knew that they were lying and they were actually Taliban allies. By ten a.m. trucks started to arrive and dismount several hundred terrorists. The tides had turned. Rob decided to back his men to their fallback position. Suddenly, their Afghan allies started yelling and pointing to the mountain, where enemy troops were charging.

The SEALs and their Afghans ran to cover as the terrorists armed with rocket-propelled grenade (RPG) executed their "shoot and maneuver" plan. It got worse as mortars started to spray and more enemy forces started to join them. He saw their Afghan ally get shot by an RPG and was saved by his backpack, falling down the cliff. But the man merely dusted himself off and yelled "Okay, USA!" to Rob. Thankfully, the Afghan managed to recover a machine gun and return fire to the enemy. Rob finally spotted Tony, their radio operator, but there was one problem – Rob had to run across the open field to reach him.

He ditched his backpack and dived to Tony, shouting just to be heard in the firefight. However, the Forward Operating Bases refused to fire in the checkpoint and instead sent random blasts which were close to worthless. The enemy continued pushing to the point that Rob could already see their faces clearly while more fighters assembled to the south for an ambush. Meanwhile, Seth and Tom informed him that intercepted radio signals confirmed a commander organizing on the mountain.

With Tony's batteries dead, Rob was forced to run back to his backpack for his batteries and return again to Tony. A bomber plane, Bones 22 confirmed bombs which would reach their target after two minutes. Rob grew increasingly frustrated from the prolonged time, the enemy fire, and the shouts of "Allahu Akbar! (God is Great!)". But he could only wait until the sound of four bombs falling from the heavens grew louder and a fireball sent shock waves as it hit the checkpoint. The shooting immediately stopped and Rob took his chance to shoot the closest, shouting terrorist and survey the battlefield.

The mortars had stopped and Rob coordinated with Tony and Bones 22 to drop bombs on the enemy lines. Four large blast lit up the entire valley two minutes later, with the enemy running around on fire. The panicking enemy frantically ran to the top of the mountain. Meanwhile, a new F-15 jet, call signed "Dude 12", had arrived and, with Rob's all-clear, dropped four five-hundred-pound bombs on the remaining escaping fighters. Several minutes later, Dude dropped four more bombs about two kilometers inside Pakistan. Now safe, Rob coordinated their extract with the helicopters overhead. As Rob watched the breathtaking scenery of the battlefield and the beautiful Konar River, he realized that he had just been in the most intense gunfight of his life with him only using forty-five bullets.

In the aftermath, the US and Pakistan investigated the incident of sending bombs in their territory. Their informants reported that they killed almost a hundred terrorists and wounded Zabit Jalil in the chest and the butt. A footage of the attack showed the Americans following the rules of engagement, saving Rob from prison. Instead, Rob received a Silver Star, the third highest military award for gallantry in combat. During Rob's Silver Star ceremony, his mother freaked after hearing the details and the danger Rob put himself in. Since he couldn't reply that it was not a big deal, Rob just promised her that he would never get another Silver Star again.

Chapter Seventeen

On April 8, 2009, the captain of the merchant ship *Maersk Alabama*, Richard Phillips, was taken hostage by four Somali pirates. The US Navy warships, despite lacking specialized rescue personnel, steamed towards the pirates and blocked their way to shore. The pirates wanted to negotiate for Phillips' life but the USS *Bainbridge* had to tow the fuel-less lifeboat.

Back home, Rob and his men were excited to participate in a high-profile hostage rescue at sea. They brainstormed all the possibilities as the negotiations in the boat went nowhere. On April 10, Rob's birthday and his daughter's Easter party at preschool, he received a call. Nicole was ready; she already knew. Rob was off to war again. With a few minutes to spare, Rob decided to stop by the 7-Eleven outside their base and buy some cigarettes just in case he needed to barter his way to freedom or get stranded in an island on his birthday.

Their gear was loaded and double-checked as the SEALs flew to the Indian Ocean for sixteen straight hours. They had to strap unwilling Navy support personnel for a tandem jump to provide additional support in the mission. Rob led a hundred and two jumpers to the speedboats which were inconveniently placed by the sun's reflection on the ocean.

They drove towards the USS *Boxer* and sailed towards the *Bainbridge*, arriving at night.

Dressed like the *Bainbridge*'s crew, they would rotate with the originals while the snipers set up their nest. The pirates, however, were growing irritable and impatient because of their drug withdrawal, seasickness, and growing confusion. Since they don't have any clear legal authority to take the pirates out in international waters, the decision fell to Walt, the SEAL officer and tactical commander with the snipers. Jonny and the snipers could see that the pirates were growing increasingly aggressive and begun "mock executions" on Captain Philipps. Jonny never realized that he would have to actually use the "Slide for Life" from BUD/S. When the three pirates' heads popped into view, Walt gave the all-clear for the snipers since they couldn't leave a survivor. Jonny had spent thousands of hours training for targets that pop up randomly and briefly that required perfect aim and instant reaction. The training paid off as the three pirates disappeared from sight. Captain Philipps was shocked but unhurt.

Meanwhile, Rob was on the *Boxer* with his boss, discussing their plans of tricking the pirates into towing them a few miles north of their Somalian village where Rob and his SEALs would be waiting.

However, while the SEALs stayed at Camp Snoopy in Qatar, Rob found Jonny depressed despite him doing something heroic, something that made SEAL Team X internationally famous. Because of that, people got envious and pissed at him, already the boss wanted to fire him.

Rob, concerned for his friend, tried to cheer up Jonny, telling him that he was a hero, that he did the best thing, and that he shouldn't listen. Eventually the head-on attacks against him died out but bad blood lingered. Rob wasn't happy about it and couldn't understand but someday, it could all come back to haunt him.

Chapter Eighteen

Reaching the worldwide headlines, Team X knew that they had become the best of the best. Thus, there were no more nerves when they got deployed again to Afghanistan to a high-altitude base, Forward Operating Base Sharana on a huge hill in Paktika Province. There was no need to homestead after the squadron before them left out the good stuff. They only get missions every third day, mostly about hunting IED makers as they rode motorcycles to Pakistan before dark.

Most of the time, the terrorists would ditch their motorcycles and took off in the fields or hills. Sometimes, they would commit suicide bombing. One time, a group of producers took the high ground on the hills, shooting down on the SEALs. Rob left his best dog, Cairo and the rest of their team as they tried to flank off the enemy. They managed to shoot down one and sent Harp, the Explosive Ordnance Disposal guy who amazed Rob for their dauntlessness, to clear the body. The body had no bombs though but had a collection of pornography videos.

However, the other half of their team radioed Rob to tell that Cairo was wounded. The Belgian Malinois had sniffed his way to the terrorist but was shot in the leg and chest. Cheese,

Cairo's handler, was unaware of what happened and immediately signaled him to return. The brave dog took a bullet from the enemy so the rest of them wouldn't have to. After killing his shooter, Cheese called a medic to treat Cairo like a human SEAL wounded in action. Everyone knew that a chest wound was hopeless. Cairo was loaded to a medevac chopper to Germany. Three days later, Team X would rejoice – Cairo had survived. He would not only fully recover but he would also help make history in the near future.

On the morning of June 30, 2009, Rob and his team would wake up to the news that Bowe Bergdahl, an American soldier with a reputation as a loose cannon, completely deserted and taken by the Taliban. The US military was desperate to get him back before he was smuggled into Pakistan. They broke their tactics as they landed helicopters right on people's front yards. On one mission, Rob almost freaked out when a group of people emerged from the house. Luckily, they were just panicking locals who gave them good information. He and his team eventually found Bergdahl's "seller" who, in fear, pointed them in a direction. Sadly, they were too late. The Taliban-allied Haqqani network was too fast to track. Some SEALs, including Rob's friend Jimmy, launched in a suspected target south of Kabul. However, well-armed and well-trained fighters engaged them, injuring Jimmy's femur and killing one of the combat dogs. The

Haqqani network kept Bergdahl captive for almost five years where he was tortured. The military eventually traded him in with five key Taliban, a high price to pay for a deserter especially if the price had already been paid in life and blood.

Chapter Nineteen

War became a routine for Rob. The spring of 2011 became his sixth year of saying goodbye to his family without any insurance that he would come back. He had also finished his seventh combat deployment with his squadron in Afghanistan and was beginning his second tour as an Assault Team Leader with Two Troop. His witty friend Paul was the other Assault Team Leader; his close friend and hero of the Captain Phillips rescue, Jonny, was his Sniper Team Leader; and Mack with his missing tooth was his number two.

Rob's number three was Nic Checque who would prove himself less than a year later in an operation to save an American doctor from Taliban fighters. As the point man, Nic was the first through the door and was shot through the head. His SEAL brother, Ed Byers, shot Nic's killer, tackled an enemy scrambling towards a gun, killed him and threw his body over the hostage while pinning another enemy to the wall with a hand to the throat. His stint would make Byers the first Team X member to be awarded with a Medal of Honor and dedicated the award to his "teammate, friend, and brother", Nic, who "died like warriors die." Nic would be posthumously awarded with the Navy Cross. In Rob's mind though, Nic was still very much alive.

Rob's troop commander was Eric Roth, a man whose strong leadership Rob admired. Their new guy, French, was adept in logistics and ran the dive trips. He had assigned them to the Courtyard Marriot, a trip that Rob found himself enjoying despite his traumatic experiences with salt water at BUD/S. It was a good trip to keep up with their combat diving skills because of the two wars' priority with close quarters combat. Rob found it nice to return to the Navy roots of worrying over pirates and training in the sea.

After learning that some positions were opened up for the Military Free-Fall Jumpmaster Course in Arizona, Paul and Rob chose Checque and Cheese for the great opportunity. The rest stayed in Miami until the evening of March 5, 2011 when Roth received a message and called the three team leaders. Jonny, Paul, Rob, and Roth were required by the command leadership for a face-to-face discussion. Something was up.

The leaders left French in charge of the dive trip but Rob couldn't still see any sense or clues about what was going on. Cheese was also called in and had to drop out of the class. They stayed in the Team Room which was an impressive place, decorated with mementos from the wars: framed photos of comrades, humans and dogs alike who have died; Neil Roberts' bent machine gun from his fall from the ridge that would soon be named after him; a bloody hood and steel handcuffs from a war criminal arrested in Bosnia; a photo from Operation Wolverine where Team X ambushed four vehicles containing nineteen al-Qaeda fighters in 2002; and a painting of the *Maersk Alabama* with the hat signed by Captain Richard Philipps; a huge black-and-red carpet with the squadron emblem; and a life-size statue of Tecumseh.

In the Commander's Conference Room, the Master Chief, Willy, told them that the mission cannot be discussed outside that room. He was also being vague and just explained that it involved getting to a secluded base station with a series of buildings similar to an Afghan compound. It was surrounded by mountains in a large bowl. Two dozen SEALs would be broken down into four teams. Rob was team leader for Team 4. The only way in, although very risky, was to insert right on top of it.

Of course, there was a lot of questions but they only received "We can't tell you yet," as replies. Since they were left out, the other members of the squadron began ignoring them as if it was a judgment of worthiness. Rob and the others felt awkward and did not want the others to be bitter for not making the cut. Not telling them information would be the salt on the raw wound. In reality, command just wanted to raise as few flags as possible.

A part of them believed it was just a joke since Team X was known for master pranks. They made up a name for the chosen twenty-four: Team Awesome which stood for something like Alienate, When Ever Suitable, Others in My Employment. Team Awesome planned as much as they could from the scarce intel. Three of the teams would handle the assault while Rob's team was assigned for perimeter security. There would be no air support and no support personnel. Team 4 would also have Cheese, the fully recovered Cairo, and a mysterious interpreter.

The meeting was adjourned to Sunday morning in a government facility in North Carolina together with the CO of SEAL Team X, the Secretary of Defense, and the CIA's Chief of Counter Terrorism PAK/AFGHAN Desk (CTC/PAD). With the remaining week left, every man in Team Awesome had to adjust to fit in support roles as well. Rob was beginning to form a suspicion though because of the CTC/PAD involvement but he couldn't quite believe his own theory.

On the ride to North Carolina, Rob confessed his suspicions, a suspicion that Roth equally shared: going after Osama bin Laden. As they sat in a large conference room, the CTC/PAD representatives briefed them about "The Pacer" who never leaves a compound in Abbottabad and never interacts with outsiders. The structure of the compound was also discussed: it was clearly arranged to keep the world out. Their suspicious were confirmed when the identity of the driver of the two vehicles was revealed: Abu Ahmed al-Kuwaiti, bin Laden's most trusted courier.

Admiral William McRaven, top commander of the Joint Special Operations Command had presented the only viable plan they could think of to President Barack Obama in early April 2011: sending in the SEALs and the helicopter pilots from the 160th Special Operations Air Regiment.

Obama agreed and gave him three weeks.

Chapter Twenty

The plan was practiced inside a life-size replica of the Abbottabad compound. Team 4 would be dropped by the helicopter, Dash 2, outside the north gate. Cheese, Cairo, and Robby the sniper would fast-rope to the roof then jump down to the third-floor balcony, where they believed bin Laden stayed. Jonny, machine gunner Mack, and Rob would hold security. Meanwhile, Dash 1 would fast-rope the primary assault team into the courtyard while the snipers on the helicopter would give them cover, making the chopper very vulnerable.

Rob believed that something seemed off with the plan so he convinced his Master Chief, Willy, to let him join the rooftop team since Jonny was already a team leader. They were made to overtrain themselves for the mission to the point that Rob developed tendonitis because of excessive fast-roping. Knowing the extreme risks they would be taking for this operation and its importance, Rob started calling themselves the Martyrs Brigade. He knew that it may be the last hours that they had alive.

On April 23, they flew home to be with their families while command prepared in Afghanistan. Nicole knew something was up even if Rob was never able to tell her much from emails since he was not allowed to be on social media. But she understood. With only a day to accomplish a lifetime of loving gestures, Rob didn't want to scare his girls so they went shopping instead. But there was no gift enough to say that he was going to die. Rob could say goodbye, kiss his kids, hold his tears for thirty seconds, and cry all the way to work. Nicole didn't have that luxury; she had to stand with her girls and give them strength by not crying ever. Rob respected her for that.

The SEALs flew to Jalalabad and met with the other SEAL Team X currently in their deployment. Because of the president's aggressive stance, they would be accompanying Rob and the Martyrs Brigade in the forward staging area in case they needed to bail them out. They watched Obama attend the White House Correspondents' Dinner broadcasted live on C-Span. They watched as Obama chuckled from bin Laden jokes. No audience would have guessed what was going on in his mind. Rob began to write his letters to his family, just in case he couldn't come back. It was extremely difficult and painful and couldn't even give them to his friends because they were all going to the mission with him and they may all die.

On Sunday, Admiral William McRaven gave them the perfect speech about the movie *Hoosiers* where Hickory High was about to play for the state championship in the biggest gym they had ever seen. The coach tells the smallest guy to measure the court and says that those were the exact same measurements of their own gym back in Hickory, only a bigger building. More people were watching but otherwise, it was exactly the same. Rob loved him for that. McRaven was born to give that speech to his Navy SEALS, whose insignia symbolized the mission: Operation Neptune's Spear.

Before being transported to their stealth Black Hawks, Rob made a phone call to his father. It had been a ritual calling him before he left on missions but his father could sense that this one was different. His father knew Rob couldn't tell him about the mission and it scared him. Rob thanked him for everything: for teaching him free throws and how to be a man. Rob ended the call with an "I love you," and boarded Dash 2.

Later, his father would sit in his truck for twenty minutes after the call, stiff with dread. By the time he made his way through the noonday crowd at Walmart, Rob was flying fast and low in a chopper on a moonless night across the Pakistan border.

Chapter Twenty-One

While flying through Pakistan, thoughts about blowing up in a helicopter began to run in the SEALs' minds. The only one happy in their team was Cairo, who was completely relaxed like a family dog on the way to a camping trip. Rob was impressed to find out that some of their guys could sleep. To keep himself relaxed, he had to count numbers and mutter ""Freedom itself was attacked this morning by a faceless coward, and freedom will be defended," lines from President George W. Bush's nation address during 9/11.

When the compound eventually came into view, the two helicopters split. Dash 1 headed to its position and fast-roped the SEALs while Dash 2 dropped off their snipers, Cheese, Cairo, and the interpreter on the north side while Rob and the others headed to the rooftop. Meanwhile, because of the high temperature and solid walls, Dash 1 failed to hover and the pilot eased the chopper to a controlled crash landing. Dash 2's pilot saw this and put them back down, with no need for verbal communication. Everyone was thankful that these were two of the best pilots in the world.

Seconds after jumping, the breacher blew up a metal gate near the northeast corner, only to find out that it was a fake door leading to a wall. The others opened the carport and entered bin Laden's house. Rob began to hear gunfire as he savored the historic moment. A martyr woman jumped in front of an al-Qaeda so one of Rob's men was forced to shoot her as well. It was definitely the right place.

The SEALs continued to clear the buildings as they heard bin Laden's three wives and seventeen children cry. Their men led the terrified women and children to one room. They may be hunting the world's most wanted man but they were going to make sure that a young girl would be safe as possible.

As they headed to the next level, they learned that Dash 1 had crashed in the front yard. With no way out, they had to hurry. With their night vision, they spotted Khalid bin Laden, Osama's armed son and his last line of defense, hiding behind a banister. The SEALs' position would be compromised if Khalid realized they were Americans. But their point man was clever. He called Khalid in his native language, Arabic and Urdu, so the confused young man poked his head around the banister. His last words were "What?" before the point man shot him in the face. Everyone else started clearing the second floor's rooms and left the point man and Rob to handle the rest of the stairs heading to the third floor.

Already spread thin, the point man took a shot at a tall figure behind the curtain but couldn't see the result. Whoever was on the third floor knew they were coming and were probably barricading themselves with weapons and suicide vests. There was no time to wait for more guys or let Cairo run ahead. Rob and the point man were impatient. They had to finish this.

The pair swiftly moved to the room as the point man lunged at the two screaming women, sacrificing himself as a blast absorber just in case they wore suicide vests. Bin Laden stood behind his youngest wife as Rob aimed above the woman's right shoulder and shot twice. The world's most wanted man dropped, his head split open, as Rob put another bullet in his head for insurance.

The wife, it turned out, was the one hiding behind the curtain earlier but was only mildly injured in the calf. Rob carried the woman over to the bed and didn't cuff her. For the first time, he saw bin Laden's youngest son who was too young to know what was happening except that it was bad. Rob pityingly picked up the crying boy who had nothing to do with all the chaos and gave him to the woman.

Rob felt blank while the other SEALs did the rest of the work. Rob and the rest found the computers, stuffing the hard drives and intel while filming everything. There were bags of opium everywhere and the SEALs rushed to carry as much stuff as they could. By then, they had overtimed and Admiral McRaven was sweating and worrying about the Pakistani military. They placed bin Laden's body in a body bag after confirming his identity from his daughters and took digital images for confirmation. The SEALs radioed McRaven and blew the downed Dash 1 as Dash 2 extracted them. Meanwhile, on the neighboring house, a guy live-tweeted the raid and blamed it on the Pakistani military.

Everything started to sink in as the other SEALs bombarded the others with one question: "Who got bin Laden?" Jonny, the hero of Captain Phillips rescue and the only one who could understand what Rob was feeling, returned the favor and calmed him down with a cigarette. Now he knows what it was like to be a hero.

Chapter Twenty-Two

For ninety minutes, the victory parade tried not to jinx themselves before the Pakistani air defense rained hell. It was like counting down for life. They couldn't believe how happy they were when the pilot finally announced that they were in Pakistan.

Reunited with the point man, the pair ran into the CIA woman. Rob gave her his gun's magazine, now short with three bullets. They walked her over the body bag of her life's work, the most wanted man in history. The movie *Zero Dark Thirty* had a much more different portrayal of the scene. Instead of walking away and tearing up, the CIA woman walked away after saying that she was out of a job.

Admiral McRaven came over and treated him like a proud father. The rest of the SEALs started to feel the euphoria as they stood around laughing by the bin Laden's corpse. With no tape measure, they just made one of the guys to lie down beside the dead body and compare the height. Later, President Obama would give McRaven a plaque with a tape measure.

The White House, CIA, and FBI gathered their reports and intel while the media started to report the mission with a lot of inaccuracies even before the president had a chance to speak. The SEALs settled down with big tubs full of food as they watched President Obama confirm bin Laden's death with no Americans harmed. SEAL Team X was in every news, placing them on the cultural radar after the perfect-for-the-movies rescues. Days later, the secretary of defense, Robert Gates, awarded the SEALs with Silver Stars. Rob had to break his promise to his mother after all. President Obama also presented them with a Presidential Unit Citation. In return, they gave Obama a framed flag they had carried on the mission signed with their call signs.

However, Rob could feel the jealousy and disapproval from his best friends. He felt uncomfortable in the spotlight, believing that it was a team effort and that the point man had done something far more heroic by tackling the women who they thought wore suicide vests. Rob began to think that the only way for the hate to disappear was if he went away even if he wanted to retire sooner. That backfired when people started to say that Rob "tried to cash in" with a book contract. He had to prove something to his teammates and he decided to join one more deployment.

On the night of August 5, 2011 in Wardak Province in Afghanistan, the Navy Special Warfare received their worst loss in history and the worst loss of American lives in a single incident of the entire Afghan conflict. Taliban RPG grenades had destroyed the helicopter Extortion 12, killing all thirty Americans, thirty-eight men aboard, and a combat dog. Rob lost his friend Robert J. Reeves in the same crash, a friend who stayed with him even after his struggles with the bin Laden mission.

The losses tore them personally and tactically. Rob was assigned to a new squadron to fill up the empty positions. It gave him a new chance to get away from the recriminations and reconsider leaving the Navy. Before Thanksgiving, Rob left for the Forward Operating Base Shank in Afghanistan. The situation there was depressing with the loss of beloved friends in addition to the winter cold and Afghan betrayers assaulting the base with mortar fire. Not spending the Christmas with his family was equally depressing as well.

It was his first time working with the Cultural Sensitivity Team (CST) who thought them Afghan culture and respecting the Quran. The female CST officers were equally tough and were good to have around. However, as they continued hunting targets almost out of boredom in Afghanistan, Rob started to feel that he had done his time.

Rob's last mission as a SEAL were some locals armed with RPGs traveling to neighboring villages. Rob and his team staged an "L" ambush to intercept their daily pattern on

Saturday. After waiting for the men to fix their broken engine and drive through, the SEALs swept through, blocking their path. Snipers started to shoot at the armed men while the rest fired their weapons. They began to sweep the scene and the machine guns, AK-47s, and grenades when one of their Afghan partners excitedly held an RPG like a child, not knowing that there was a bullet hole in the charge. That was the reason Rob wanted out.

Chapter Twenty-Three

After four hundred combat missions, minefields, flying hostile missions through the missile defense system of a nuclear power, and getting pinned by a superior force in a dead-end valley, Rob still found leaving the Navy as the scariest. In his sixteen and a half years in service, he received two Silver Stars, four Bronze Stars with Valor, a Joint Service Commendation Medal with Valor, three Presidential Unit Citations, and a Navy/Marine Corps Commendation Medal with Valor. He also had a mortgage, no pension, no college degree, no job, and a deadline on August 23rd for his kid's health care. Thank you for your service.

As a civilian, he learned that being a Navy SEAL is the only part of his life: those challenges he overcame and the priceless comradery with his SEAL brothers. Before he had killed anybody famous, being a SEAL was his best experience in the world. But he had to keep growing and move on to the next phase: life.

Because he had ended the life of the world's most hunted man, Rob gained the ability to influence. There were veterans who had tougher jobs than him: facing minefields everyday, strolling through IED-wired streets, spending months in the valleys of Afghanistan who found themselves with nothing. There were the thousands who lost families and loved ones in

9/11. Rob wanted to raise awareness and help.

Anonymously, in the summer of 2015, he donated his uniform that he had worn on the mission to the National September 11 Memorial & Museum in New York. After that, he was brought to the stage in front of the people who lost their loved ones and was asked to say something. Rob wasn't prepared but as he started talking, he felt this powerful connection. It was his first time publicly telling his story of the bin Laden mission. People crowded around him to say how much his story meant, that they were not afraid anymore because Rob told them the truth, that bin Laden was really dead.

A man approached him with his grandson whose father died in 9/11 to tell him that every day, his grandson would ask him why God did this. The man would always reply that God didn't do this, the devil did. And with a tear running down his cheek and a defiant gleam in his eyes, the man told Rob that he had killed the devil.

Up to now, Rob never knew if being the one who killed Osama bin Laden was the best thing that ever happened to him or the worst. He was confident, though, that it all happened for a reason and he was committed to make the most of it.

Conclusion

The Operator is a book of war, of peace, of sacrifice and heroism, of victory and loss, of friendship, of willpower, and of heroism. Robert O'Neill's personal accounts as a Navy SEAL provides readers with a view of what it is like to be a soldier and a man whose shots changed the world.

The flow of his stories and the conversational way it was written gives the military topics a new perspective. The action is captivating and thrilling at the same time. Rob's experiences as his time in the Navy SEALs is comparable to an exclusive sneak peek that news reports and movies mostly fail to provide: the individuality and brotherhood of these soldiers, their inner thoughts and opinions during their missions, and their humanity. Most often, the media would portray them as tough commandos but *The Operator* provides a different point of view of the soldiers' lives while they were not doing missions: pranks, jokes, and their own way of having fun.

Growing up in Butte, Montana never gave Robert "Rob" O'Neill the idea of joining the military. His father had instilled in him the obsessive drive to keep striving. Hilariously, it was his girlfriend's father who indirectly convinced him to serve his country instead of spending the rest of his life acting like a fool. By that time though, his purpose was to impress the town and Rob never gave a second thought about combat or death. Despite his inability to swim, the naïve young man signed for the Navy. He rigorously trained for the SEAL (Sea, Air, and Land) screening test as he enlisted.

Navy boot camp wasn't like the movies since they only studied Navy courtesies, all kinds of folding, and marching. Rob decided to take the SEAL screening test before he got fat. He failed his first try because the Navy immunization shots made him weak. By his second try, the side effects had gone and Rob's training paid off as he passed as one of four from five hundred takers. But that extremely difficult test was nothing compared to the Basic Underwater Demolition/SEAL (BUD/S) training. To improve himself, Rob took the risk and retook the screening test ten times.

Rob checked in as BUD/S Class 208. He and his friend Matthew Parris were temporarily housed in the "X Division" with the quitters who kept complaining and blaming others until they were moved to the heart of the compound.

Before the actual BUD/S training, they had to undergo Physical Training Rehabilitation and Remediation (PTRR) for preliminary training. It was a harder version of the screening exams and more stressful because of the screaming instructors. Some still failed and Matthew almost became one of them. Rob and the rest "graduated" from PTRR and received their green BUD/S helmets, stenciled with their name.

Phase One was like torture as instructors sprayed them with frigid water, made them run miles in the beach and plunge themselves in the Pacific Ocean, ordered hundreds of push-ups and ab exercises while they yelled at them. The obstacle course was high, daunting, and almost life-threatening. Matthew fell from one of the courses, losing his chance in becoming a SEAL, but later became an excellent skydiver. Another test, the "drown-proofing", had the trainees' hands and feet tied up as they tried to swim in the pool or retrieve something underwater. The beehive was more deadly because of the challenge of staying afloat in a deep, crowded pool. There were also four-mile timed runs and impassable room inspections specially sabotaged by instructors. It was designed to pressure and stress the trainees.

Rob, who didn't want to see his father's name on the "quitter line," refused to give up. He started to enjoy the training as he strived to beat records. There was also one instructor, Instructor A, who motivated the trainees to continue. Rob and the other survivors eventually learned techniques and became stronger. Rob even managed to pass a room inspection as they played a prank that the instructors joined in. To survive BUD/S, he realized, one must place BUD/S as his top priority and refuse to quit. They all thought it was hell but Hell had not yet begun.

Hell Week started in induced mayhem so instructors could see how they handle stress and confusion. The next evolution was paddling towards surf zones and carrying the rafts across deadly rocks in repetition. Now, they had to carry their 320-pound rubber raft everywhere as weight was added until their arms and heads gave out. In the Steel Pier, they were required to lie down as instructors sprayed them with hoses. The training overstressed their ligaments and chafed their body. Most of the time, they were cold, exhausted and in pain. There was virtually no sleep for sixty hours. The instructors were looking for men who do not blame the others for taking their own weight and kept fighting.

By the last night of Hell Week, the instructors treated the trainees nicer as they finished their "Around the World", a complete circumnavigation of the island while carrying their boats. That also included plunging into a sewage mud pit. At last, Hell Week was finished and the survivors received their new brown shirts. His parents even came to celebrate Rob's milestone with the help from Instructor A.

Phase Two included the usual evolutions, hydrographic reconnaissance, WWII-era Underwater Demolition Team tactics, diving physics lessons, and Pool Week which required them to run a mile while carrying heavy scuba tanks. In the Pool Competency Test, instructors rigged their gear in almost impossible knots to train them how to handle life-threatening diving situations. Rob failed his first try because of an impossible knot but successfully passed the second after unknotting them thrice. Rob found diving underneath ships and propellers enjoying. Later, he would also pass a rigged 5.5-nautical-mile swim twice.

Phase Three was actually fun for Rob because it included Naval shooting ranges, camping trips, and blowing stuff up. During their BUD/S training finale, Rob was chosen by Team Two, his dream team. The following Friday, thirty-three survivors from Class 208's two hundred students graduated. Rob realized that it wasn't about race, or size, musculature, or I.Q. In the end, it was sheer determination and strength of the mind. After graduation, Rob celebrated with his family and attended Basic Airborne School where he earned his "blood wings."

Rob discovered that the SEALs had a special bond of camaraderie and equality. The legendary SEALs had legendary humor. Personally, Rob would be inspired by the holder of the "O" course record, Neil Roberts, because he was exactly the man Rob aspired to be. When he passed the final oral exam, Rob felt immense pride as he received his Trident pin and was now officially a Naval Special Warfare Operator.

As a SEAL, Rob started to get his own share of first nautical deployments, helicopter crashes, Europe tours, interrogation, minefields, and action. In the early 2000s, their mission would make the headlines worldwide as they caught a Russian oil tanker smuggling Iraqi oil. In the late summer of 2001, Rob and his team watched a passenger jet slice the first tower of the World Trade Center in New York, killing hundreds of innocents. That moment changed their lives. Rob would also be informed about Neil Robert's death in Operation Anaconda, where he fell from his chopper and fought terrorists to the death. His rescue was too late. Although reinforcements captured the summit that would eventually be named after him, it costed Robert's and six other Americans' lives. When his death reached Rob, war finally became real.

To fight bin Laden and his terrorists, Rob trained to join SEAL Team X. They practiced skydiving in Arizona where Rob almost died from a parachute malfunction. They didn't report it however, and it would later haunt Rob. They also had close quarters battle (CQB) training and Survival,

86

Evasion, Resistance, and Escape - two valuable trainings for infiltrating a terrorist location.

Rob was sent home after learning that his wife was in labor. Despite him having a new daughter, he was still determined to avenge Robert's death. He completed training in December 2004 and was chosen by the squadron responsible for Operation Anaconda and Robert's supposed rescue. He would find out that these combat-hardened men were great pranksters.

His first combat mission was in Jalalabad, Afghanistan. His first mission included arresting a Saudi Arabian terrorist. With all his training, Rob learned that there was no need for stress during operations. A dozen more missions followed without a single shot fired from both sides.

Rob recounts the "Lone Survivor" incident, where four SEAL snipers were spotted by the terrorists in the Korengal "Valley of Death". Heavily outgunned and outnumbered, they made their final stand as they called SOF Quick Reaction Force. Helicopters immediately took off but the leading chopper was shot down with most of SEAL Team Ten inside it. Only Marcus Luttrell survived but he was badly injured. Fortunately, he took refuge with the locals. Several Special Forces volunteered to aid the rescue, among them was Rob. They hiked for days, fighting with dehydration, drowsiness, and Taliban. Thankfully, they were contacted by the local villagers and were able to extract Luttrell.

Team X joined the considerably more dangerous fight in Iraq. They were determined to introduce new tactics and techniques. Every night, the SEALs used the darkness to their advantage; stealth and night vision allowed them to effectively put down targets. They steadily worked from the bottom of the terrorist pyramid to reach the No.1 target, the bombing and massacre mastermind: Abu Musab al-Zarqawi. Those were Rob's first kills. He felt no remorse for the men who dedicated their life destroying Western culture, men who celebrated after bombing a tourist hotel full of innocents.

Rob's family were making large sacrifices as well with Rob spending 325 days each year away from home, in a constant risk of death. Still, his friends and teammates, the super sniper Greg, Lance with his bad luck, and their brave combat dogs always had his back. Team X would experience a lot from their deployments, eventually becoming the most lethal and stealthy team in modern history.

In the Spring of 2007, Rob and Nicole would have a second daughter. On one of their missions, Rob had to kill three children's terrorist parents right in front of them. Guilty, he personally accompanied the children, who were the same age

88

as his own, to their aunt.

By May of 2007, the number of SEALs and American soldiers in Iraq were growing as the numbers of terrorists were decreasing. Commander Rich, as a considerably humble SEAL, believed that working under the Army Special Forces in Baghdad would benefit his men and the overall operation. It allowed the SEALs to learn more and experience more. They would also reach the headlines as "Ninjas and they came with lions" when the SEALs and their combat dogs infiltrated an IED producer in a peninsula, killing nineteen terrorists and freeing the villagers. Sometimes though, the SEALs would get cocky and risk some missions. Rob knew that emotions should not cloud their judgement in making crucial decisions.

Still, the SEALs weren't always so lucky. Rob began to lose his beloved teammates one by one during combat operations or parachute failure. Their beloved combat dogs who died courageously in battle were also mourned like their own brothers. One particular death that haunted Rob was his friend Lance's. He had an extreme case of bad luck but the reason for his death was a parachute malfunction – the same malfunction that Rob had encountered and failed to report. They would honor Lance's death by exactly following his "If I Die" wishes.

Rob would receive a Silver Star for leading his men in a huge battle against Zabit Jalil's Talibans. Although heavily outgunned, he managed to call in an air strike that destroyed their checkpoint and killed a hundred terrorists in the Afghan/Pakistan border.

On April 10, 2009, Rob and Team X participated in the *Maersk Alabama* hijacking where four Somali pirates took Captain Richard Phillips hostage. His friend, Jonny the sniper managed a miraculous shot that saved the captain. However, Jonny would earn jealousy and bad attitude from his own team members. Concerned for his friend, Rob comforted Jonny, telling him that he did the best thing and should not listen to the others.

The rising action of Rob's life started when they received a call from command on the evening of March 5, 2011. Something different and highly confidential was up. Command briefed two dozen SEALs to infiltrate a compound in Abbottabad without giving any more details. It confused them and the other members were already showing signs of jealousy because of the secrets. Rob and the others formed the suspicion that they were going to assassinate Osama bin Laden because of the CIA's CTC/PAD involvement.

Their suspicions were right. They trained for hours in a life-size replica of the compound with all the scenarios that they could think of. They trained for perfection. Knowing the extreme risks, Rob tried to express a lifetime of loving gestures without saying anything to his family. As he wrote his letters for them just in case he couldn't come back, Rob felt terrible and painful.

On that fateful Sunday of May 2011, Admiral William McRaven reminded them that the mission just had more audience but was just like any other. Before riding the Black Hawks, Rob called his father to thank him for everything. When they finally reached Abbottabad that night, the choppers successfully dropped the SEALs and the combat dog Cairo. They proceeded to clear the building and eliminate bin Laden's son and last line of defense: Khalid. Rob would find himself with just their point man as they entered the third floor. The pair swiftly moved as the point man lunged at two women, sacrificing himself in case they wore suicide vests. Bin Laden stood behind his youngest wife as Rob shot him thrice.

It was done. The world's most wanted man was dead.

Rob felt blank while the other SEALs did the rest of the work and packed all intel. On their ride home, he could already feel the curiosity and disapproval from the others. Jonny, the hero of Captain Phillips rescue and the only one who could understand what Rob was feeling, returned the favor and calmed him down with a cigarette. Now he knows what it was like to be a hero.

The White House, CIA, and FBI gathered their reports and intel as President Obama confirmed bin Laden's death. Seal Team X was in every news as America erupted into celebration and joy. The SEALs received Silver Stars and a Presidential Unit Citation. Still, Rob could feel the backlash from his teammates. To prove them wrong, Rob joined another deployment. It gave him a new chance to get away from the recriminations and reconsider leaving the Navy. But Rob thought he was becoming sloppy and felt like he had done his time.

After four hundred combat missions in his sixteen and a half years of service, Rob received two Silver Stars, four Bronze Stars with Valor, a Joint Service Commendation Medal with Valor, three Presidential Unit Citations, and a Navy/Marine Corps Commendation Medal with Valor. Before the bin Laden incident, Rob felt like being in the SEALs was his best experience but he knew he had to move on with life.

As the person who shot the three bullets that changed the

world, Rob decided to use his influence to support the 9/11 victims and help the veterans who faced a similar problem: an unclear future. In the summer of 2015, he donated his uniform to the National September 11 Memorial & Museum. He also gave an impromptu speech to the people who lost their loved ones and family. Rob felt a powerful connection. Afterwards, people thanked him and told him how much his story meant.

Rob never knew if killing Osama bin Laden was the best or the worst thing that ever happened to him. Still, it happened for a reason and he was committed to make the most of it.

In the end, *The Operator* provides readers with lessons that is not only applicable as a Navy SEAL, but as a normal citizen in everyday life as well. The SEALs' unwavering determination and ability to adapt in any stress and pain is inspiring. In the end, excellence would be given to those who had the strongest will. These brave men could be set as an example to people: ready to defend freedom and justice against any odds.

One of the most important eye-openers in the book was the great sacrifice of soldiers. They risk their lives continuously in foreign lands to defend innocents. Yet, even with all their sacrifice, they are sometimes treated poorly or found themselves with nothing after retirement. Doing something heroic and brave doesn't always mean that one would be treated like one. This is why Rob's determination to use his influence to help the veterans and victims alike is a noble cause.

Over all, *The Operator* lives up to its award as a *New York Times* Bestseller.

Final Thoughts

Hey! Did you enjoy this book? We sincerely hope you thoroughly enjoyed this short read and have gotten immensely valuable insights that will help you in any areas of your life.

Would it be too greedy if we ask for a review from you?

It takes 1 minute to leave 1 review to possibly influence 1 more person's decision to read just 1 book which may change their 1 life. Your 1 minute matters and we value it and thank you so much for giving us your 1 minute. If it sucks, just say it sucks. Period.

FREE BONUS

P.S. Is it okay if we overdeliver?

Here at Abbey Beathan Publishing, we believe in overdelivering way beyond our reader's expectations. Is it okay if we overdeliver?

Here's the deal, we're going to give you an extremely valuable cheatsheet of "Accelerated Learning". We've partnered up with Ikigai Publishing to present to you the exclusive bonus of "Accelerated Learning Cheatsheet"

What's the catch? We need to trust you... You see, we want to overdeliver and in order for us to do that, we've to trust our reader to keep this bonus a secret to themselves. Why? Because we don't want people to be getting our exclusive accelerated learning cheatsheet without even buying our books itself. Unethical, right?

Ok. Are you ready?

Simply Visit this link: http://bit.ly/acceleratedcheatsheet

We hope you'll enjoy our free bonuses as much as we've enjoyed preparing it for you!

Free Bonus #2: Free Book Preview of Summary:

Outliers

The Book at a Glance

Outliers: The Story of Success is critically-acclaimed author and The New Yorker writer Malcolm Gladwell's third best-selling non-fiction book that talks about how people succeed in life through crafted cultural background, impeccable timing and presented opportunities. Published in 2008, the book is compartmentally divided into two parts, the first part talking about opportunities that are presented to successful people and the latter about how legacies can make someone successful. Gladwell carefully examines and narrates how a person's environment, infused with high intensities of motivation and passion affects their possibility of being truly successful and faithfully tells others' success stories often using back-to-back chronologies through the likes of The Beatles, Bill Gates and even the hockey players of The Medicine Hat Tigers. Though *Outliers* fairly abstains from previous books "*The Tipping Point*" and "*Blink*" because of its social narrative, *Outliers* has been praised for being pleasurable to read and might as well have great timing for this generation to understand and comprehend.

Malcolm Timothy Gladwell, born in 1963 in Fareham,

Hampshire, England to Joyce and Graham Gladwell is a staff writer for The New Yorker since 1996 and has written five New York Times Bestseller books, *The Tipping Point: How Little Things Can Make A Big Difference* (2000), *Blink: The Power of Thinking Without Thinking* (2005), *Outliers: The Story of Success* (2008), *What the Dog Saw: And Other Adventures* (2009) and David and *Goliath Underdogs, Misfits, and the Art of Battling Giants* (2013). He also hosts podcast *Revisionist History*.

The Gladwells moved from England to Canada when the writer was only 6, and graduated at the University of Toronto, Trinity College with a degree in History in 1984. Gladwell worked with Washington Post as a reporter for a decade with articles on science and business before joining the "New Yorker" magazine. He moved to New York shortly after to try his hand at journalism and found international success as a writer and penned all five books to become successful worldwide. Time magazine has named Gladwell as one of its "100 Most Influential People" in 2005 and has received the first "Award for Excellence in the Reporting of Social Issues" by the American Sociological Association in 2007.

Introduction

The Roseto Mystery: "These people were dying of old age. That's it."

This introduction laboriously introduces us to the Rosetansten men, how they have lived desperately in the mountains of Roseto Valtefore, in a small Italian province of Foggia until such time when they discovered greener pastures in the land across the ocean and moved to America seeking a better life. In Pennsylvania, the Rosetansten men learned how to carry out jobs, work in services and make their way around the city. Led by a priest by the name of Father Pasquale de Nisco, the Rosetansten men were encouraged to plant their own crops, take spiritually enriched lives and build harmonious relationships which would later prove extremely beneficial. Initially called "Little Italy", the citizens of the city renamed it to Roseto, after their origin.

In this overture, Gladwell creatively uses *The Roseto Mystery* to tell the tale of how the residents of Rosetansten men merely had half the rate of heart attack cases in comparison to its neighboring communities. In 1964, a study was published in the Journal of the American Medical Association and examined the reason for the community's near immunity to heart disease and contributed it to the underlying reasons of being a remarkably close-knit community that induced respect and support for another, therefore suggesting that the affirmation of family and social relationships subsidized how a person's personal health would turn out.

Led by physician Stewart Wolf, experts from sociology and medicine came to Roseto to examine and investigate what contributed to the outstanding health of its residents and performed different conclusions ranging from a well-balanced diet, exercise and even good sets of genes. However, this all proved to be counterfactual, as they have found out that the fundamental reason for the outstanding health in the town was due to the peaceful, abetting and close-knit qualities of the community to which Gladwell craftily uses as a debut to his full feature story and herald his book's mission and suffuses his conclusion with that of Stewart Wolf's to prove that success is indeed created and not purely coincidental.

Gladwell creatively uses the Roseto Mystery as a preliminary guide to how this book was going to take its claim, by using the story of the Rosetansten men and giving it a bigger theatre stage. He pushes forward the idea that a little town in Pennsylvania can ward off diseases – even cardiac illnesses just by forming amicable relationships with one another.

In the modern world today, this kind of analysis plays a big role in society as it clears the pathway of an animated discovery into the world of communication and unison amongst humanity, to the point of being immune to major diseases.

Chapter 1

The Matthew Effect: "For unto everyone that hath shall be given, and he shall have abundance. But from him that hath not shall be taken away even that which he hath." - Matthew 25:29

"The Matthew Effect", the first chapter of *Outliers*, where he divides the chapter into six bite-sized bullets, commences with Gladwell's account of the 2007 Memorial Cup hockey championship game between the Medicine Hat Tigers and the Vancouver Giants to which the latter emerged as winners. Gladwell meticulously describes how the game went and effortlessly cites a previous research study performed by Canadian psychologist Dr. Roger Barnsley.

He tells us a story of how Dr. Roger Barnsley and his wife watched a game of hockey, wherein they see these blinking lights that signal a bright idea that leads them to the relative age effect theory Barnsley therefore crafts into a realistic approach.

In this relative age effect theory, Barnsley notices a high percentage of ice-hockey players being born during the first months of the year, from January to March and thoroughly concludes how this greatly affects the performance of a sports team, particularly in the games of hockey, soccer and rugby. In the first chapter of the *Outliers*, Gladwell ceremoniously rides on the idea and creates it as his ticket to show the readers of how age and maturity plays a big role in success. To further rationalize, players born in the early part of the year have a higher chance of being prepared and develop skills faster than those born during the latter part of the year therefore corresponding it to a higher rate of ascendancy. He further explains that being an athlete does not pay attention to dynasty, or money because being in the major league is not something you can easily purchase or is controlled by certain sovereignty. In fact, being an athlete meant you needed to have the ability, the skill, the passion and the dedication to at least render countless of hours training and doing related activities to further enhance your prowess in the field. He creates an imaginary skill pyramid for his readers to conceptualize, where those who participate in this game go up a ladder until they reach the top most part where they find true success.

The second bullet of this chapter begins as Gladwell demonstrates what outliers are; by definition and by how he portrays them, painting an overall view for his readers as he starts to set the stage for the next chapters. He guarantees that as you read and progress throughout his book, he will introduce to you various examples of the different people who have grown into outliers and have become successful. He creates a relatable topic when he describes how regular citizens love to read about tycoons, millionaires, celebrities and follow how their life in the public eye unfolds. He makes a slight jab of irony on how these regular people buy all the articles and autobiographies these famous people make, in an effort to know they made it big and possibly follow suit, enveloped in that dream to become millionaires and billionaires in the sound future. However, in a swift move, Gladwell disputes what is normal to most – which people can rise from nothing and become great. To our author, people become great because of the thousands of hours they spent on perfecting their skill, and eventually becoming an expert in that field. Gladwell goes on to convince his readers that parentage and patronage does have major contributions to a person's success, alluding that a person's environment is vital to his success because internal and external factors do have a sizable impact on a person's wellbeing that eventually transcends to how he performs.

Gladwell also cites two economists Kelly Bedard and Elizabeth Duey who looked into the relationship between scores in Mathematics and Science, contributing to his theory that those born early in the year scored better in comparison to those who were born later in the year. With this, he gives enough justification that although Dr. Barnsley has cited his theory and making athletes as examples, Gladwell advocates that it doesn't only happen in the world of sports, in fact, it happens across all industries, we just don't notice it enough.

He finishes the first chapter going back to the ice-hockey game story and introduces us to Gord Wasden, father of Medicine Hat Tigers player Scott Wasden and how in an interview he has mentioned that his son was born on January 4 – the perfect hockey eligibility, rendering him bigger than kids his age. He ends this chapter with a conclusion that if Scott Wasden was born later in the year, he would have less chance playing in the game and a bigger chance watching from the bench.

Read More...

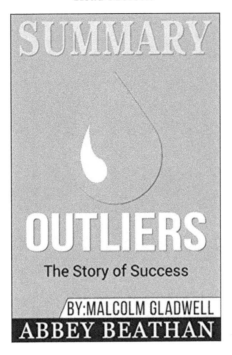